Introduction to TYPE® in ORGANISATIONS

Individual Interpretive Guide

Third Edition

EUROPEAN ENGLISH VERSION

Sandra Krebs Hirsh
Jean M. Kummerow

About the Authors

Sandra Krebs Hirsh, MA, MAIR, is principal of Sandra Hirsh Consulting, a Minneapolis-based management consulting firm. Her type is ENFP.

Jean Kummerow, PhD, is a consulting psychologist and principal of Jean Kummerow & Associates, a St. Paul-based management consulting firm. Her type is ESTJ.

Distributed under licence from the Publisher, CPP, Inc., 1055 Joaquin Road, 2nd Floor, Mountain View, California, USA 94043.

OPP Ltd
Elsfield Hall
15–17 Elsfield Way
Oxford
OX2 8EP
UK

Tel: +44 (0)845 603 9958
www.opp.com

ISBN 978 1 85639 100 9

Contents

What Is the MBTI®?

This booklet is designed to help you understand your results on the *Myers-Briggs Type Indicator®* (MBTI®) personality inventory and their applications in organisational settings. The MBTI provides a useful method for understanding people by looking at eight personality preferences that everyone uses at different times. These eight preferences are organised into four opposite pairs. When you take the Indicator, the four preferences (one from each pair you identify as being most like you) are combined into what is called a *type*.

The four pairs of preferences, or dichotomies, describe four activities:

- Energising – how a person is energised, either through Extraversion (E) or Introversion (I)
- Perceiving – what a person pays attention to, either through Sensing (S) or Intuition (N)
- Deciding – how a person decides, either through Thinking (T) or Feeling (F)
- Living – the lifestyle a person adopts, either through Judging (J) or Perceiving (P)

Some characteristics of each preference are presented in the table below.

Some Characteristics of Each of the Four Scales

Energising	**Extraversion (E)** Preference for drawing energy from the outside world of people, activities and things	**Introversion (I)** Preference for drawing energy from one's internal world of ideas, emotions and impressions
Perceiving	**Sensing (S)** Preference for taking in information through the five senses and noticing what is actual	**Intuition (N)*** Preference for taking in information through a "sixth sense" and noting what might be
Deciding	**Thinking (T)** Preference for organising and structuring information to decide in a logical, objective way	**Feeling (F)** Preference for organising and structuring information to decide in a personal, values-oriented way
Living	**Judging (J)** Preference for living a planned and organised life	**Perceiving (P)** Preference for living a spontaneous and flexible life

* To avoid duplication and confusion, the letter "N" is used for Intuition because the letter "I" signifies Introversion.

The MBTI has been applied as a tool for many years by a variety of users around the globe, including those in

- Small businesses and large multinational corporations
- Service industries and manufacturing concerns
- Consulting and training services
- Government at all levels
- Established firms and new entrepreneurial ventures
- Educational and health care institutions

In general, the MBTI functions as a tool that helps people in organisations

- Understand themselves and their behaviours
- Appreciate others in order to make constructive use of individual differences
- Approach problems in different yet healthy ways and thus be more productive

Specifically, organisations use the MBTI to

- Make the most of their human resources
- Utilise individuals' natural strengths
- Improve teamwork
- Understand and adapt to differences in leadership/ management style
- Enhance effective communications between supervisors, peers, employees and customers
- Assist in career development
- Resolve conflict
- Coach individuals
- Design training activities
- Recognise employees' unique contributions
- Develop skills in creativity, time management and stress management

The MBTI was developed in the United States by a mother-and-daughter team, Katharine Briggs and Isabel Myers. The Indicator is based on the work of C. G. Jung's theory of psychological type.

In order to understand your results, remember that the MBTI

- Describes rather than prescribes; therefore, it is used to open possibilities, not limit options
- Identifies preferences, not skills, abilities or competencies
- Assumes that all preferences are equally important, valuable and necessary
- States that all preferences can be used by each person
- Is well documented with thousands of scientific studies conducted during a 50-year period
- Has ongoing research to support its application

Because the results on the MBTI are subject to a variety of influences (ie work tasks, family demands and/or cultural norms), they need to be treated with caution and individually verified. You will want to determine the type that comes closest to describing you. This probably is the same type as reported on the MBTI, although this is not always the case. You can use this booklet to help you find the personality type that best fits you.

The MBTI Preferences

The eight MBTI preferences are explained in three ways:

- By presenting a list of vocabulary words commonly associated with each preference
- By examining the effects of the preferences in work situations
- By looking at how the preferences affect communication

As you read pages 2–4, you may find it helpful to tick or circle all those words and phrases that apply to you and see which preferences describe you best.

Vocabulary

Energising (orientation of energy)

Extravert (E)	Introvert (I)
external/exterior	internal/interior
outside thrust	inside pull
talk thoughts out	keep thoughts in
breadth	depth
involved with people, things	work with ideas, thoughts
interaction	concentration
action	reflection
do–think–do	think–do–think

Perceiving (perception)

Sensing (S)	Intuition (N)
present orientation	future possibilities
what is real	what could be
practical	theoretical
facts	inspirations
perfecting established skills	learning new skills
utility	novelty
step-by-step	insight-by-insight
the five senses	the sixth sense, a hunch

Deciding (judgment)

Thinking (T)	Feeling (F)
logical system	value system
head	heart
objective	subjective
justice	mercy
criticism	compliment
principles	harmony
reason	empathy
firm but fair	compassionate

Living (orientation towards the outside world)

Judging (J)	Perceiving (P)
decide about information	pay attention to/gather information
regulate	flow
control	adapt
settled	tentative
run one's life	let life happen
set goals	seek options
closing off	opening up
organised	flexible

Effects of Preferences in Work Situations

Extraversion
- Like participating actively in a variety of tasks
- Are often impatient with long, slow jobs
- Are interested in the activities of their work and in how other people do them
- Act quickly, sometimes without thinking
- Find phone calls a welcome diversion when working on a task
- Develop ideas by discussing them with others
- Like having people around and working in teams

Introversion
- Like quiet and private space for concentration
- Tend to be comfortable working on one project for a long time without interruption
- Are interested in the facts and/or ideas behind their work
- Like to think before they act, sometimes to the point of not acting
- Find phone calls intrusive when concentrating on a task
- Develop ideas alone through reflection
- Like working by themselves or occasionally in small groups

Sensing
- Like using experience and standard ways to solve problems
- Enjoy applying skills already perfected
- Seldom make errors of fact, but may ignore inspirations
- Like to do things with a practical bent
- Like to present the details of their work first
- Prefer continuation of what is, with fine tuning
- Proceed step-by-step or piece-by-piece, accurately estimating the time needed

Intuition
- Like solving new, complex problems
- Enjoy the challenge of learning something new
- Seldom ignore insights but may overlook facts
- Like to do things with an innovative bent
- Like to present an overview of their work first
- Prefer change, sometimes radical, to continuation of what is
- Proceed in bursts of energy, following their inspirations as time goes by

Thinking
- Use logical analysis to reach conclusions
- Can work without harmony, concentrating instead on the task
- Upset people inadvertently by overlooking their emotions
- Decide impersonally, sometimes paying insufficient attention to people's wishes
- Tend to be firm-minded and ready to offer criticism
- Look at the principles involved in the situation
- Want recognition after task requirements are met or exceeded

Feeling
- Use values to reach conclusions
- Work best in harmony with others, concentrating on the people
- Enjoy meeting people's needs, even in small matters
- Let decisions be influenced by their own and other people's likes and dislikes
- Are sympathetic and dislike, even avoid, telling people unpleasant things
- Look at the underlying values in the situation
- Want appreciation throughout the process of working on a task

Judging
- Work best when they can plan their work and work to their plan
- Enjoy organising and finishing tasks
- Keep the focus on what needs to be completed, ignoring other things that come up
- Feel more comfortable once a decision has been made about a thing, situation or person
- Decide quickly in their desire for closure
- Seek structure and schedules
- Use lists to prompt action on specific tasks

Perceiving
- Want flexibility in their work
- Enjoy starting tasks and leaving them open for last-minute changes
- Want to include as much as possible, thus deferring needed tasks
- Feel comfortable staying open to experiences, not wanting to miss anything
- Postpone decisions because of a search for options
- Adapt to changing situations and feel restricted with too much structure
- Use lists to remind them of possible things to do when time allows

Adapted from *Introduction to Type* (1st ed.), by Isabel Briggs Myers, CPP, Inc., 1962.

Preferred Methods of Communication

Extraversion

- Communicate energy and enthusiasm
- Respond quickly without long pauses to think
- Converse about people, things and ideas in the external environment
- May need to moderate expression
- Seek opportunities to communicate with groups
- Prefer face-to-face over written communication, voice mail over e-mail
- In meetings, like talking out loud to build their ideas

Introversion

- Keep energy and enthusiasm inside
- Pause and reflect before responding
- Thoroughly consider ideas, thoughts and impressions
- May need to be drawn out
- Seek opportunities to communicate one-to-one
- Prefer written over face-to-face communication, e-mail over voice mail
- In meetings, verbalise ideas that have been thought through

Sensing

- Like evidence (facts, details and examples) presented first
- Want practical and realistic applications shown, with any relationships between the facts clearly explained
- Rely on direct experience to provide information and anecdotes
- Use an orderly step-by-step approach in conversations
- Like suggestions to be straightforward and feasible
- Refer to specific examples
- In meetings, follow the agenda

Intuition

- Like global schemes, with broad issues presented first
- Want to consider future possibilities and challenges
- Use insights and imagination as information and anecdotes
- Rely on a roundabout approach in conversations
- Like suggestions to be novel and unusual
- Refer to general concepts
- In meetings, use the agenda as a starting point

Thinking

- Prefer to be brief and concise
- Want the pros and cons of each alternative to be listed
- Can be intellectually critical and objective
- Convinced by cool, impersonal reasoning
- Present goals and objectives first
- Use emotions and feelings as secondary data
- In meetings, seek involvement with the task first

Feeling

- Prefer to be personable and in agreement
- Want to know an alternative's impact on people and values
- Can be interpersonally appreciative and accepting
- Convinced by personal authenticity
- Present points of agreement first
- Consider logic and objectivity as secondary data
- In meetings, seek involvement with people first

Judging

- Want to agree on schedules, timetables and reasonable deadlines
- Dislike surprises and want advance warning
- Expect others to follow through and count on this
- State their positions and decisions as final
- Want to hear about results and achievements
- Focus on purpose and direction
- In meetings, concentrate on task completion

Perceiving

- Willing to discuss timetables but resist tight deadlines and unchangeable schedules
- Enjoy surprises and adapt to last-minute changes
- Expect others to respond to situational requirements
- Present their views as tentative and modifiable
- Want to hear about options and opportunities
- Focus on autonomy and flexibility
- In meetings, concentrate on the process being used

Adapted from *Talking in Type* by Jean M. Kummerow, Center for Applications of Psychological Type, 1985.

Preference Groupings

Your type is determined by your responses to the questions on the MBTI. Since each of the eight preferences are represented by a letter (E, I, S, N, T, F, J or P), a four-letter code can be used as a shorthand for indicating type. For example, ESTJ suggests a person who is energised by the external world (E), whose preferred way of perceiving incoming information is Sensing (S), whose way of deciding is Thinking (T), and who adopts a Judging (J) style of living.

An individual type is the combination of one preference from each of the four preference pairs, or dichotomies. When the four dichotomies are combined in all possible ways, sixteen types result. These sixteen types are displayed on a type table. Once you are familiar with how the type table is constructed, you can look at the data and quickly form impressions of or hypotheses about the group that is displayed on the table. The type table is arranged as follows:

- **Introversion** in the top two rows and **Extraversion** in the bottom two rows
- **Sensing** in the two left columns and **Intuition** in the two right columns
- **Thinking** in the two outer columns and **Feeling** in the two inner columns
- **Judging** in the top and bottom rows and **Perceiving** in the inside rows

People who work with type like to group the preferences together in different ways that are meaningful to them and to their task. Here are three common groupings of the preferences: by quadrants of the type table, by function pairs (or columns) of the type table, and by temperaments.

Type Table

	S	S	N	N	
I	ISTJ	ISFJ	INFJ	INTJ	J
I	ISTP	ISFP	INFP	INTP	P
E	ESTP	ESFP	ENFP	ENTP	P
E	ESTJ	ESFJ	ENFJ	ENTJ	J
	T	F	F	T	

The Four Quadrants

One combination often used to describe personality type relates to the *quadrants* of the type table. These quadrants combine the energising preferences (E–I) and the perceiving preferences (S–N) and result in IS, ES, IN and EN quadrants. The quadrants are often used to describe leadership, learning and work styles as well as corporate culture and ways of handling change.

Preference Grouping by Quadrants (IS, IN, ES, EN)

IS	IN
ES	EN

	IS – Thoughtful Realist	IN – Thoughtful Innovator
Leadership:	Through attention to what needs doing	Through ideas to what needs doing
Work environment:	▪ Quiet, reflective, thoughtful ▪ Hours that are regular and scheduled ▪ Administrative focus:-procedures are followed and exceptions noted ▪ Reliance on written words and policies	▪ Quiet, reflective, thoughtful ▪ Hours that can be sporadic ▪ Quasi-academic focus: independent of procedures ▪ Reliance on written words and research
Individual focus:	Practical considerations	Intangible thoughts and ideals
Learning focus:	What can be applied to current or anticipated needs	Learning for learning's sake; for the joy of creating something new
Learning process:	By reading and observing	By reading and reflecting
Organisational focus:	Continuity, such as in administration and accounting	Vision, such as in research and development
Change:	Comes from seeing the difference between what should be preserved and what could be changed	Comes internally from their visions of the future
Motto:	"Let's keep it!"*	"Let's think about it differently!"*

	ES – Action-Oriented Realist	EN – Action-Oriented Innovator
Leadership:	Through action, doing	Through enthusiasm
Work environment:	▪ Energetic, outgoing, active ▪ Hours that are regular and scheduled ▪ Implementation focus: time is spent out and about doing what works ▪ Reliance on spoken words leading to action	▪ Energetic, outgoing, active ▪ Hours that can be sporadic with bursts of energy ▪ Cutting edge focus: time is spent out there trying new things ▪ Reliance on spoken words leading to possibilities
Individual focus:	Practical actions	Systems and relationships
Learning focus:	What is relevant that will help me do my job better now	What is engaging and fun that feeds my creativity and insight
Learning process:	By doing	By talking/acting through ideas
Organisational focus:	Results, such as in sales, production and manufacturing	Change, such as in marketing, promotions and new ventures
Change:	Comes from getting things to run more effectively and efficiently	Comes from trying something different or novel
Motto:	"Let's do it!"*	"Let's change it!"*

*Mottos are excerpts from *Organizational Tendencies* by Earle C. Page, Center for Applications of Psychological Type, 1985.

There may be some creative tension between the diagonals (IS versus EN and IN versus ES). For example, while the ISs are saying "If it ain't broke, don't fix it!" the ENs say "If it ain't broke, break it!" The INs may be so busy envisioning a possibility that they overlook the steps involved in its implementation – a forte of the ESs.

All four perspectives are needed and are valuable to organisations. When one or more perspectives are missing, organisational members can use the chart on page 6 to see what or where to supplement their view to ensure an optimal outcome. This does not mean that an organisation needs to add a "missing type" to its group; rather, members should be encouraged to use all preferences.

The Four Function Pairs

These combinations of preferences (ST, SF, NF, NT) are also known as the *function pairs* and correspond to the columns of the type table. They are often related to communication style, problem solving, career choice and organisational culture.

All four perspectives add value to an organisation. When one or more perspectives are missing, people can use the chart below to supplement their view to ensure an optimal outcome.

Preference Grouping by Function Pairs (ST, SF, NF, NT) or Type Table Columns

ST SF NF NT

	ST	SF	NF	NT
People who prefer:	Sensing + Thinking	Sensing + Feeling	Intuition + Feeling	Intuition + Thinking
Focus on:	What is; the facts	What is; the facts	What could be; the possibilities	What could be; the possibilities
Contribute:	Policies and procedures	Internal and external customer service	Ideals worth striving for	Theoretical concepts
Have as a goal:	Efficiency	Helping others	Empowerment	Mastery
Ask questions about:	How will it be done, by when, and how much does it cost?	Who will it affect, who will do it, and how?	How will it be communicated and who will it impact?	What is the latest and most relevant theory or strategy?
Like computers for:	Keeping track of data	Keeping track of data, especially data relating to people	Aiding growth and development of self and others	Modelling and simulating
Experience conflict:	When work is not done correctly	When people disagree	When values are ignored or crossed	When principles are incorrect or faulty
Reduce conflict by:	Having the structures in place	Meeting people's needs	Articulating values clearly	Making sure the principles are sound
Want teams to focus on:	Bottom line	Offering support	Giving encouragement	Systems
May be found in these types of organisations:	Government, production, construction	Service, health care, education	Communication, arts, counselling and development	Start-up technologies, scientific, academic

The Four Temperaments

A third useful way of grouping preferences is referred to as temperament. Temperament

- Is based primarily on observable clusters of behaviour, which may be seen as "activity patterns"
- Describes differences in people noticed and documented throughout history in a variety of cultures, including Greek and Native American
- Has four variations, not sixteen, and therefore the themes are even easier for people to grasp quickly
- Can be determined by the MBTI

Temperaments can be found in the type table on the right.

Effects of Combinations of Preferences by Temperaments (SJ, SP, NF, NT)

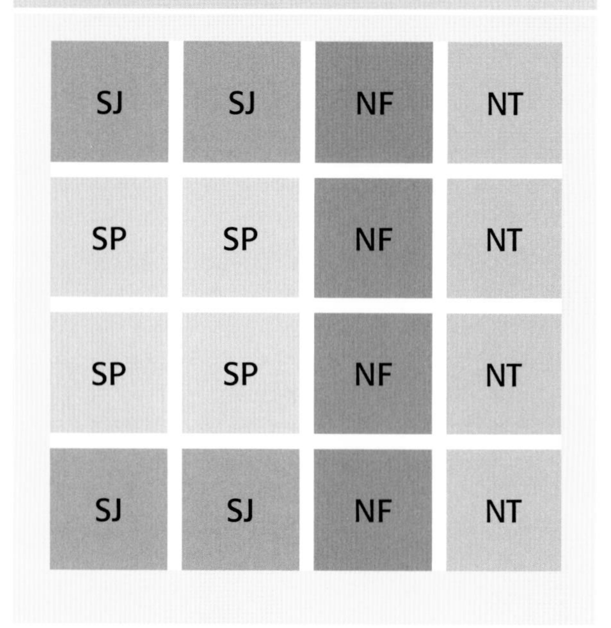

Preference Grouping by Temperaments (SJ, SP, NF, NT)

Temperament	SJ – Guardians	SP – Artisans	NF – Idealists	NT – Rationals
Leadership style:	Traditionalist, stabiliser consolidator	Troubleshooter, negotiator, fire-fighter	Catalyst, spokesperson, energiser	Visionary, architect of systems, builder
Work style:	Has a sense of duty responsibility, loyalty and industry	Acts with cleverness and timelessness	Persuades people about values and inspirations	Adds ingenuity and logic to ideas and actions
To do best work, they need:	Knowledge of the goal and what they're supposed to do to get there	Freedom to do things as they see fit	Personal meaning and congruence with who they are	Intriguing models to challenge their imagination
Learning style:	Step-by-step, with preparation for current and future utility	Active involvement to meet current needs	Personalised and imaginative ways of self-awareness	Impersonal and analytical process for personal mastery
Want others to see them as:	Hard-working and reliable	Resourceful and risk taking	Authentic and inclusive	Competent and logical
Acknowledged for contributing:	Administrative expertise, timely output	Expeditious handling of the out-of-the-ordinary and the unexpected	Something unique or a special vision of possibilities	Strategic analysis of complex issues
Want to be known for their:	Dependability	Spontaneity that includes a spirit of play	Ability to inspire others	Expertise
Can get into trouble by being:	Too bureaucratic	Too expedient	Too idealistic	Too competitive

Descriptions of the Sixteen Types

Below are single words, arranged in alphabetical order, often used in self-descriptions by people of each of the sixteen types. Longer type descriptions appear on the pages referenced next to the types.

In reading the individual type descriptions, keep in mind that there are no "good" or "bad" types. The MBTI identifies preferences, not abilities or skills. As expressed in the descriptions that follow, each type has something to offer and something to learn that could enhance its contribution to the organisation.

Short Descriptions of the Sixteen Types

ISTJ *(page 10)*

dependable	realistic
exacting	reliable
factual	reserved
logical	sensible
organised	steadfast
practical	thorough

ISFJ *(page 14)*

accommodating	patient
detailed	practical
devoted	protective
loyal	quiet
meticulous	responsible
organised	traditional

INFJ *(page 18)*

compassionate	intense
conceptual	intimate
creative	loyal
deep	methodical
determined	reflective
idealistic	sensitive

INTJ *(page 22)*

analytical	organised
autonomous	original
determined	private
firm	systems-minded
global	theoretical
independent	visionary

ISTP *(page 11)*

adaptable	logical
adventurous	practical
applied	realistic
expedient	resourceful
factual	self-determined
independent	spontaneous

ISFP *(page 15)*

adaptable	modest
caring	observant
cooperative	sensitive
gentle	spontaneous
harmonious	trusting
loyal	understanding

INFP *(page 19)*

adaptable	gentle
committed	idealistic
curious	imaginative
deep	intimate
devoted	loyal
empathetic	reticent

INTP *(page 23)*

autonomous	precise
cognitive	self-determined
detached	sceptical
independent	speculative
logical	spontaneous
original	theoretical

ESTP *(page 12)*

activity-oriented	outgoing
adaptable	persuasive
adventurous	pragmatic
alert	quick
easygoing	spontaneous
energetic	versatile

ESFP *(page 16)*

adaptable	outgoing
casual	playful
cooperative	practical
easygoing	sociable
enthusiastic	talkative
friendly	tolerant

ENFP *(page 20)*

creative	imaginative
curious	independent
energetic	original
enthusiastic	restless
expressive	spontaneous
friendly	versatile

ENTP *(page 24)*

adaptive	original
analytical	outspoken
challenging	questioning
clever	resourceful
enterprising	strategic
independent	theoretical

ESTJ *(page 13)*

decisive	organised
direct	practical
efficient	responsible
gregarious	structured
logical	systematic
objective	task-focused

ESFJ *(page 17)*

conscientious	responsible
cooperative	responsive
harmonious	sociable
loyal	sympathetic
personable	tactful
plan-oriented	traditional

ENFJ *(page 21)*

appreciative	idealistic
congenial	loyal
diplomatic	organised
energetic	personable
enthusiastic	responsible
expressive	supportive

ENTJ *(page 25)*

challenging	objective
controlled	opinionated
decisive	plan-oriented
energetic	straightforward
logical	strategic
methodical	tough-minded

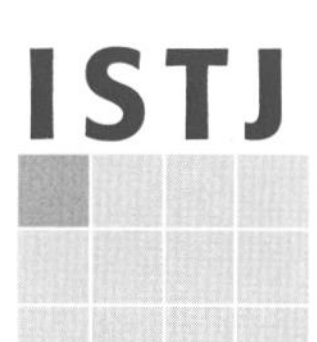

ISTJ

Introverted Sensing with Thinking

ISTJs are thorough, exacting, systematic, hard-working and careful with detail. They enjoy working within organisations to improve procedures and processes, remaining loyal through both good and bad times.

Contributions to the Organisation

- Get things done steadily and on schedule
- Concentrate on details and are careful about managing them
- Have things at the right place at the right time
- Can be counted on to honour commitments and follow through
- Work within organisational structure comfortably

Order of Preferences*

1 Sensing
2 Thinking
3 Feeling
4 Intuition

* *See pages 26–29 for further explanation.*

Leadership Style

- Use experience and knowledge of the facts to make decisions
- Build on reliable, stable and consistent performance
- Respect traditional, hierarchical approaches
- Reward those who follow the rules while getting the job done
- Pay attention to immediate and practical organisational needs

Problem-Solving Approach

- Want to be thoroughly grounded in the facts (S) analysed in a logical framework (T)
- May need to consider the impact on people (F) and search for more possibilities and other meanings (N) for optimal results

Preferred Learning Style

- Presented in a concrete and sequential style
- Practical with applications that are useful now

Preferred Work Environments

- Contain realistic, hard-working people focused on facts and results
- Provide long-term security
- Reward a steady pace and those who meet deadlines
- Utilise structure with systematic methods
- Are task-oriented and firm-minded
- Offer quiet and orderly settings
- Allow privacy for uninterrupted work

Potential Pitfalls

- May overlook the long-range implications in favour of day-to-day operations
- May neglect interpersonal niceties
- May become rigid in their ways and perceived as inflexible and less open to innovation
- May expect others to provide the same level of detail and conform to the same operating procedures

Suggestions for Development

- May need to pay attention to wider, future ramifications of problems in addition to present realities
- May need to consider the human element and communicate deserved appreciation
- May need to try fresh alternatives to avoid ruts
- May need to develop patience for those who communicate differently or who bypass standard operating procedures

ISTP

Introverted Thinking with Sensing

ISTPs are pragmatic, aware of facts, expedient, realistic, and not likely to be convinced by anything but reasoning. They enjoy working independently, relying on logic and resourcefulness to solve immediate organisational problems.

Contributions to the Organisation

- Act as troubleshooters, rising to meet the needs of the occasion
- Function as walking storehouses of information in areas in which they have an interest
- Figure out practical ways to get things done, overcoming obstacles in the way
- Remain calm during crises and thus have a settling effect on others
- Add expertise to projects where they have technical skills

Order of Preferences*

1 Thinking
2 Sensing
3 Intuition
4 Feeling

* *See pages 26–29 for further explanation.*

Leadership Style

- Lead through action and by setting an example
- Prefer that everyone be treated as equals and pull his or her own weight
- Respond quickly when trouble arises, using the most expedient techniques
- Manage others loosely and prefer minimal supervision themselves
- Operate from clear, logical principles

Problem-Solving Approach

- Want to use their internal logic to structure problems and solutions (T) while attending to the facts and specifics (S)
- May need to consider other possibilities (N) and the impact on people (F) for optimal results

Preferred Learning Style

- Lively and entertaining
- Useful content and practical applications that are interesting to them

Preferred Work Environments

- Contain action-oriented people focused on the immediate situation
- Are project-oriented and task-focused
- Pay attention to what is logical
- Reward a quick response to problems
- Allow for hands-on experience
- Offer freedom to do the job as they see fit
- Foster independence and autonomy

Potential Pitfalls

- May keep important things to themselves and thereby appear unconcerned
- May seem to lack follow-through, moving on before their initial effort bears fruit
- May conserve efforts, be overly expedient and take short cuts
- May appear indecisive, lacking in interest, energy and follow-through

Suggestions for Development

- May need to open up and share concerns and information with others
- May need to develop perseverance or communicate changes in direction
- May need to plan and put in the effort necessary to achieve desired results
- May need to develop methods of setting and keeping goals

ESTP

Extraverted Sensing with Thinking

ESTPs are action-oriented, pragmatic, resourceful and realistic individuals who prefer to take the most efficient route. They enjoy making things happen now and typically find a way through difficult situations.

Contributions to the Organisation

- Negotiate and seek compromise to move things along
- Keep things lively; make things happen
- Take a realistic and direct approach
- Embrace risk in a calculated way
- Notice and remember factual information

Order of Preferences*

1 Sensing
2 Thinking
3 Feeling
4 Intuition

See pages 26–29 for further explanation.

Leadership Style

- Take charge readily in crises
- Persuade others to see their point of view
- Have a direct and assertive style
- Move along the most expedient route
- Seek action and immediate results

Problem-Solving Approach

- Want to make a realistic and concrete assessment of the situation (S) and logically analyse the next steps (T)
- May need to consider the impact on people (F) and search for alternate possible views (N) for optimal results

Preferred Learning Style

- Active, hands-on, trial and error in determining what works
- Practical and focused on something they can apply now

Preferred Work Environments

- Contain lively, results-oriented people who value firsthand experience
- Have rules, but space is given for deviations
- Allow time for fun
- Provide for flexibility in doing the job
- Have a technical orientation with all the latest equipment
- Are physically comfortable
- Respond to the needs of the moment

Potential Pitfalls

- May appear demanding, blunt and insensitive when acting quickly
- May focus too much on the immediate and miss the wider implications of their actions
- May sacrifice follow-through by moving on to the next problem
- May get caught up in outside activities, such as sports and other hobbies

Suggestions for Development

- May need to curb their task focus and take account of the feelings of others
- May need to look beyond the quick fix, plan ahead, and consider the wider ramifications
- May need to complete the tasks at hand
- May need to keep work and play in the proper perspective

ESTJ

Extraverted Thinking with Sensing

ESTJs are logical, analytical, decisive and tough-minded, using concrete facts in systematic ways. They enjoy working with others well in advance to organise the details and procedures to get the job done.

Contributions to the Organisation

- See, point out and correct flaws in advance
- Provide criticisms of programmes in a logical, objective way
- Organise the process, product and people to achieve goals
- Monitor to determine that the tasks are done correctly
- Follow through in a step-by-step way

Order of Preferences*

1 Thinking
2 Sensing
3 Intuition
4 Feeling

See pages 26–29 for further explanation.

Leadership Style

- Seek leadership directly and take charge quickly
- Apply and adapt past experiences to solve problems
- Get to the core of the situation swiftly and directly
- Decide and implement quickly
- Act as traditional leaders who respect the hierarchy, achieving within the system

Problem-Solving Approach

- Want to logically analyse and control situations (T) based on pertinent facts and relevant details (S)
- May need to look at the broader picture (N) and the impact on people and themselves (F) for optimal results

Preferred Learning Style

- Active, hands-on and done in a structured way
- Practical and focused on something they can use

Preferred Work Environments

- Contain hard-working people determined to get the job done properly
- Are task-oriented and committed
- Offer organisation and structure
- Have team projects
- Provide stability and predictability
- Focus on efficiency and productivity
- Reward meeting goals

Potential Pitfalls

- May decide too quickly and pressure others to do so too
- May not see the need for changing things that they believe are already working
- May overlook the interpersonal niceties in getting the job done
- May be overtaken by their emotions when they ignore their own feelings and values for too long

Suggestions fo

- May nee includ
- May nee benefits c
- May need appreciatio
- May need to to reflect on a

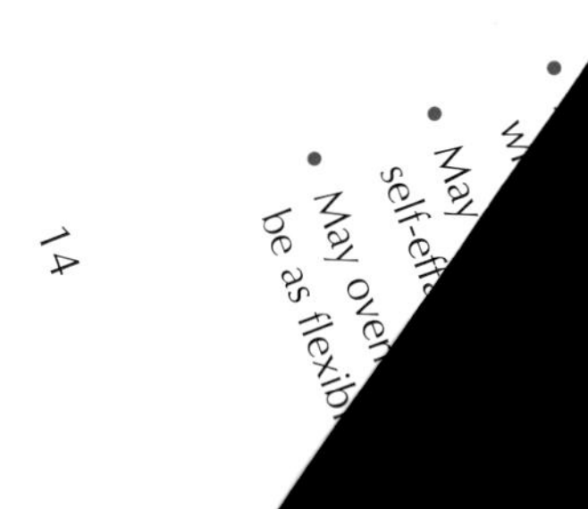

ISFJ

Introverted Sensing with Feeling

ISFJs are sympathetic, loyal, considerate and kind, and will go to any amount of trouble to help those who need it. They enjoy providing behind-the-scenes support and encouragement.

Contributions to the Organisation

- Take the practical needs of each person into account
- Use follow-through skills in carrying out organisational goals
- Are patient, even painstaking, and responsible with detail and routine
- Expend efforts willingly to serve others
- Have things at the right place at the right time

Order of Preferences*

1 Sensing
2 Feeling
3 Thinking
4 Intuition

** See pages 26–29 for further explanation.*

Leadership Style

- May be reluctant to accept leadership at first, but will step in when needed
- Expect themselves and others to comply with organisational needs and structures
- Use own personal influence behind the scenes
- Follow traditional procedures and rules conscientiously
- Use eye for detail to achieve practical results

Problem-Solving Approach

- Want to be thoroughly grounded in the facts (S), especially those that apply to people and values (F)
- May need to step back, consider what is logical (T), and search for more possibilities and other meanings (N) for optimal results

Preferred Learning Style

- Structured and quiet with enough time to commit material to memory
- Practical and focused on what will help people

Preferred Work Environments

- Contain conscientious people working on well-structured tasks
- Provide security and predictability
- Are clearly structured and organised
- Maintain calm and quiet, with some privacy
- Require a thorough approach with adequate follow-through
- Are personalised, kind and considerate
- Offer a service orientation

Potential Pitfalls

- May be overly cautious, especially about the future
- May not be seen as sufficiently tough-minded [illegible]hen presenting their views to others
- [illegible] be undervalued because of their quiet, [illegible]cing style
- [illegible]ely on their own experience and not [illegible]e as the situation or others require

Suggestions for Development

- May need to work at taking calculated risks and seeing the future in positive, global terms
- May need to develop more assertiveness and be more direct
- May need to learn to publicise and spotlight their own accomplishments
- May need to work at remaining open to other ways of doing things

ISFP

Introverted Feeling with Sensing

ISFPs are gentle, considerate and compassionate toward those in need of help; they use an open-minded, flexible approach. They enjoy working cooperatively and harmoniously, but often on their own individual tasks.

Contributions to the Organisation

- Respond to the needs of each person in the organisation as they arise
- Act to ensure others' well-being
- Infuse a particular joy into their work
- Bring people and tasks together by virtue of their cooperative nature
- Pay attention to how people are treated

Order of Preferences*

1 Feeling
2 Sensing
3 Intuition
4 Thinking

See pages 26–29 for further explanation.

Leadership Style

- Lead reluctantly, preferring a team approach, often acting as coordinator
- Use personal loyalty as a means of motivating others
- Offer more praise and support than criticism
- Rise to the occasion and adapt to what is needed
- Gently persuade by tapping into others' good intentions

Problem-Solving Approach

- Want to reflect on what really matters to themselves and others (F) with a pragmatic view of facts and experiences (S)
- May need to consider other interpretations and possibilities (N) and decide about things more objectively (T) for optimal results

Preferred Learning Style

- Quiet with opportunities to experience things directly
- Practical and focused on what will help people

Preferred Work Environments

- Contain cooperative people quietly enjoying their work
- Allow for private space
- Have people who are compatible
- Provide flexibility and security
- Are aesthetically appealing
- Include courteous coworkers
- Seek practical outcomes

Potential Pitfalls

- May be too trusting and unwilling to question
- May not criticise others when needed in order to avoid conflict
- May focus only on the present reality, missing things in their fuller context
- May be overly self-critical and too easily hurt

Suggestions for Development

- May need to develop more scepticism in analysing others' information
- May need to learn how to give negative feedback to others and manage conflict
- May need to develop a wider and more future-oriented perspective
- May need to be more assertive with others and more appreciative of themselves

ESFP

Extraverted Sensing with Feeling

ESFPs are friendly, outgoing, fun-loving, likeable and naturally drawn towards others. They enjoy working in groups with other lively, fast-paced people, as well as offering alternatives based on common sense.

Contributions to the Organisation

- Bring energy, enthusiasm and a spirit of cooperation
- Present a positive image of the organisation
- Offer action, excitement and fun
- Link people, information and resources
- Accept and deal with others as they are, even treating them generously

Order of Preferences*

1 Sensing
2 Feeling
3 Thinking
4 Intuition

* *See pages 26–29 for further explanation.*

Leadership Style

- Lead through the promotion of goodwill and team-work
- Prefer managing initial steps of a project
- Defuse tense situations by putting people at ease
- Make things happen by focusing on immediate problems
- Facilitate effective interactions among people

Problem-Solving Approach

- Want to make a realistic and concrete assessment of the situation (S), especially about people (F)
- May need to add objectivity (T) and a long-range vision of what else might happen (N) for optimal results

Preferred Learning Style

- Interactive with ample time to talk through new information
- Practical with content they can try out to see what works

Preferred Work Environments

- Contain energetic and easygoing people focused on present realities
- Are lively and action-oriented
- Foster a fast pace
- Include people who are adaptable and spontaneous
- Emphasise being harmonious, friendly and appreciative
- Are upbeat and sociable
- Look attractive and colourful

Potential Pitfalls

- May overemphasise subjective data in an effort to maintain harmony
- May not reflect on what is at hand before jumping in
- May spend too much time socialising and neglect tasks
- May not always finish what they start

Suggestions for Development

- May need to include logical implications in their decision making in order to depersonalise conflict
- May need to plan ahead when managing work
- May need to balance task and socialising time
- May need to work on project and time management

ESFJ

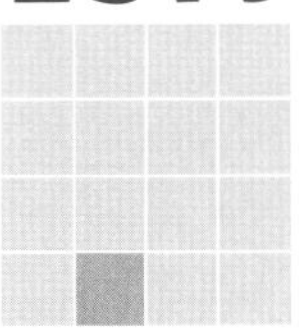

Extraverted Feeling with Sensing

ESFJs are helpful, tactful, compassionate and orderly. They place a high value on getting along with others and enjoy organising people and projects to help complete the tasks at hand.

Contributions to the Organisation

- Bring a service orientation and attitude
- Pay close attention to each person's needs, desiring to please
- Complete tasks in a timely and accurate way
- Respect rules and authority
- Handle day-to-day operations efficiently

Order of Preferences*

1 Feeling
2 Sensing
3 Intuition
4 Thinking

See pages 26–29 for further explanation.

Leadership Style

- Lead through personal attention to others
- Gain cooperation through good relationships
- Keep people well informed
- Set an example of hard work and follow-through
- Uphold organisational traditions

Problem-Solving Approach

- Want to consider values and the impact on people (F) as well as pertinent facts and useful details (S)
- May need to identify other interpretations and meanings (N), and to logically and dispassionately analyse them (T) for optimal results

Preferred Learning Style

- Structured, participative and personable with ample time to talk through new information
- Practical material with known applications

Preferred Work Environments

- Contain conscientious, cooperative people oriented toward helping others
- Are goal-oriented with helpful procedures in place
- Reward organisation and efficiency
- Encourage friendships
- Are appreciative and outgoing
- Foster interpersonal sensitivity and caring
- Include both facts and values

Potential Pitfalls

- May avoid conflict and sweep problems under the carpet
- May ignore their own priorities because of a desire to please others
- May prescribe what they assume is best for others or the organisation
- May not always take the time to step back, be objective and see the bigger picture

Suggestions for Development

- May need to learn how to pay attention to differences and manage conflict
- May need to take account of their personal needs and wants
- May need to listen more objectively to what is really needed
- May need to consider the logical, global implications of their decisions

INFJ

Introverted Intuition with Feeling

INFJs trust their visions, are compassionate and insightful, and quietly exert influence. They enjoy working alone or in compatible small groups, using their inspirations for people's growth and development.

Contributions to the Organisation

- Provide future-oriented insights directed at serving human needs
- Follow through on commitments
- Work with integrity and consistency
- Use periods of solitude and concentration to come up with creative ideas
- Organise complex interactions between people and tasks

Order of Preferences*
1 Intuition
2 Feeling
3 Thinking
4 Sensing

*See pages 26–29 for further explanation.

Leadership Style

- Lead through their vision of what is best for others and the organisation
- Win cooperation rather than demand it
- Utilise a quiet, intense and persistent course of action toward strategic objectives
- Work to make their inspirations real
- Motivate others towards their ideals in a determined manner

Problem-Solving Approach

- Want to identify an internal vision of what is possible (N), especially in relation to people and values (F)
- May need to include objective views of their vision of the future (T) as well as the details needed to make it a reality (S) for optimal results

Preferred Learning Style

- Individualised and reflective, so depth can be attained
- Focused, structured and complex with an emphasis on concepts and relationships

Preferred Work Environments

- Contain people strongly focused on ideals that make a difference to human well-being
- Provide opportunities for creativity and expressing their values
- Encourage harmony and consideration
- Have smooth-running processes respectful of people's needs
- Reward personal insights
- Foster quiet with time and space for reflection
- Are organised and plan-focused

Potential Pitfalls

- May find their ideas overlooked and underestimated
- May not be forthright with criticism
- May be reluctant to intrude upon others and thus keep too much to themselves
- May operate with single-minded concentration for what they believe is best for the future

Suggestions for Development

- May need to develop political understanding and assertiveness skills when presenting their ideas
- May need to learn to give constructive feedback to others on a timely basis
- May need to solicit feedback and suggestions along the way
- May need to relax and be more open to the present situation

INFP

Introverted Feeling with Intuition

INFPs are open-minded, idealistic, insightful and flexible individuals who want their work to contribute to something that matters. They enjoy working by themselves or in small groups where they can be creative.

Contributions to the Organisation

- Communicate and persuade with their ideals
- Draw individuals together around a common purpose
- Work to find matches for people in organisations
- Seek new ideas and possibilities for the organisation
- Quietly push an organisation to uphold its values

Order of Preferences*

1 Feeling
2 Intuition
3 Sensing
4 Thinking

See pages 26–29 for further explanation.

Leadership Style

- Take a facilitative approach
- Prefer unique leadership roles rather than conventional ones
- Work independently towards their vision
- Are more likely to praise than to criticise others
- Encourage people to act on their ideals

Problem-Solving Approach

- Want to reflect on what is really important to them and others (F) and to seek out creative possibilities (N)
- May need to gather factual data (S) and decide about things more objectively (T) for optimal results

Preferred Learning Style

- Quietly engaging their interests, and imaginatively presented
- Flexible and focused on their own and others' development

Preferred Work Environments

- Contain pleasant and committed people focused on important values
- Have a cooperative atmosphere with a lightness of spirit
- Allow privacy as well as working with others
- Provide flexibility with minimal routine
- Are non-bureaucratic
- Foster calm and quiet
- Allow time and space for reflection

Potential Pitfalls

- May delay completion of tasks because of perfectionism
- May try to please too many people at once
- May not adjust their ideals to the facts and logic of the situation
- May spend more time in reflection than in action

Suggestions for Development

- May need to learn to work with what is rather than searching for an ideal response
- May need to develop more tough-mindedness and a willingness to say "no"
- May need to take account of facts and logic along with their personal values
- May need to develop and implement action plans

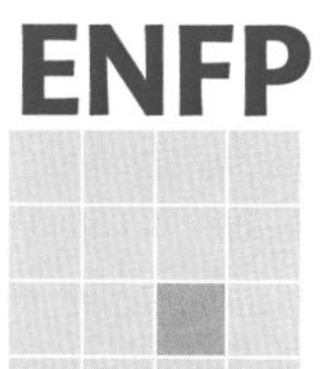

ENFP

Extraverted Intuition with Feeling

ENFPs are enthusiastic, insightful, innovative, versatile and tireless in their pursuit of new possibilities. They enjoy working in teams to bring about change related to making things better for people.

Contributions to the Organisation

- See the need for and initiate change
- Focus on possibilities, especially for people
- Energise and persuade others through their contagious enthusiasm
- Add creativity and imagination to projects and actions
- Appreciate and acknowledge others

Order of Preferences*

1 Intuition
2 Feeling
3 Thinking
4 Sensing

** See pages 26–29 for further explanation.*

Leadership Style

- Lead with energy and enthusiasm
- Prefer to take charge of the start-up phase
- Communicate and often become spokespersons for worthy causes
- Work to include and support people while allowing for their own and others' autonomy
- Pay attention to what motivates others and encourage them to act

Problem-Solving Approach

- Want to explore creative possibilities for growth (N) that fit with their values (F)
- May need to apply logic dispassionately (T) and consider the relevant facts and details (S) for optimal results

Preferred Learning Style

- Active, experiential and imaginative
- Interesting content, whether or not it has practical applications

Preferred Work Environments

- Contain imaginative people focused on human possibilities
- Allow for sociability and flair
- Relish participative atmospheres with different people and perspectives
- Offer variety and challenge
- Encourage ideas
- Are flexible, casual and unconstrained
- Mix in fun and enjoyment

Potential Pitfalls

- May move on to new ideas or projects without completing those already started
- May overlook relevant details and facts
- May overextend and try to do too much
- May procrastinate while searching for the best possible answer

Suggestions for Development

- May need to set priorities based on what is most important and then follow through
- May need to pay attention to and focus on key details
- May need to learn to screen tasks and say "no" rather than trying to do what is initially appealing
- May need to apply project and time management skills to meet goals

ENFJ

Extraverted Feeling with Intuition

ENFJs are interpersonally focused, understanding, tolerant, appreciative and facilitators of good communication. They enjoy working with others on a variety of tasks focused on the development of people.

Contributions to the Organisation

- Bring strong ideals of how organisations should treat people
- Enjoy leading and facilitating teams
- Encourage cooperation
- Communicate organisational values
- Like to bring matters to fruitful conclusions

Order of Preferences*

1 Feeling
2 Intuition
3 Sensing
4 Thinking

See pages 26–29 for further explanation.

Leadership Style

- Lead through personal enthusiasm and praise
- Take a participative stance in managing people and projects
- Respond to followers' needs while trying to put everyone at ease
- Challenge the organisation to make actions congruent with values
- Inspire change that is beneficial to people

Problem-Solving Approach

- Want to consider values and the impact on people (F) by identifying a future vision (N)
- May need to include more factual data (S) and to logically and dispassionately analyse it (T) for optimal results

Preferred Learning Style

- Interactive and cooperative with many opportunities to talk about what is important to them
- Well-structured with much encouragement

Preferred Work Environments

- Contain individuals focused on changing things for the betterment of others
- Are people-oriented and social
- Encourage support and appreciation
- Have a spirit of harmony and empathy
- Encourage self-expression
- Are settled and decisive
- Seek responsiveness and order

Potential Pitfalls

- May idealise others and suffer from blind loyalty
- May sweep problems under the carpet when in conflict
- May ignore tasks in favour of relationship issues
- May take criticism personally and be overly self-critical

Suggestions for Development

- May need to recognise the limitations of people and guard against unquestioning loyalty
- May need to learn to manage conflict productively
- May need to pay as much attention to the details of the task as to the people involved in the task
- May need to suspend self-criticism and listen carefully to objective information

Introverted Intuition with Thinking

INTJs are independent, individualistic, single-minded and determined individuals who trust their vision of possibilities regardless of universal scepticism. They enjoy working by themselves on projects that are complex.

Contributions to the Organisation

- Provide theoretical insights and design skills
- Organise ideas into action plans
- Work to remove obstacles to goal attainment
- Have strong ideas of what the organisation can be
- Push everyone to understand the system as a whole with its complex interaction among parts

Order of Preferences*

1 Intuition
2 Thinking
3 Feeling
4 Sensing

See pages 26–29 for further explanation.

Leadership Style

- Drive themselves and others to attain the organisation's goals
- Act strongly and forcefully in the field of ideas
- Can be tough-minded with self and others
- Conceptualise, create and build new models
- Are willing to relentlessly reorganise whole systems when necessary

Problem-Solving Approach

- Want to use their internal vision for strategies, systems and structures (N), which they have objectively determined (T)
- May need to include the input of others (F) and the details needed to make their visions a reality (S) for optimal results

Preferred Learning Style

- Individualised, reflective and in-depth in areas of interest to them
- Intellectual, theoretical and with the big picture first

Preferred Work Environments

- Contain decisive, intellectually challenging people focused on implementing long-range visions
- Allow independence and privacy for reflection
- Are efficient
- Include competent and productive people
- Encourage and support autonomy
- Provide opportunities for creativity
- Are task-focused and deliberate

Potential Pitfalls

- May appear so unyielding that others are afraid to approach or challenge them
- May keep their ideas to themselves for too long, believing others see things the same way
- May have difficulty letting go of impractical ideas
- May be so task-focused that they pay scant attention to others' contributions

Suggestions for Development

- May need to solicit feedback and suggestions on both their personal style and their ideas
- May need to communicate with and involve others in their ideas and strategies early on
- May need to face reality when the data do not support their ideas
- May need to be sure others' contributions are encouraged and acknowledged

INTP

Introverted Thinking with Intuition

INTPs are rational, curious, theoretical and abstract, preferring to organise ideas rather than situations or people. They enjoy working alone with ample autonomy for their own ideas and methods.

Contributions to the Organisation

- Design logical and complex systems
- Demonstrate expertise in tackling intricate problems
- Add short- and long-range intellectual insight
- Apply logic, analysis and critical thinking to issues
- Concentrate on core issues

Order of Preferences*

1 Thinking
2 Intuition
3 Sensing
4 Feeling

* *See pages 26–29 for further explanation.*

Leadership Style

- Lead through conceptual analysis of problems and goals
- Apply logical systems thinking
- Want to lead other independent types while seeking autonomy for themselves
- Relate to people based on expertise rather than position
- Seek to interact at an intellectual rather than an emotional level

Problem-Solving Approach

- Want to use their internal logic to structure problems and solutions (T) while searching for possible options (N)
- May need to pay attention to present reality and data (S) as well as to the needs and wants of others (F) for optimal results

Preferred Learning Style

- Individualised with no set beginning or end, following their own interests in depth
- Broad, conceptual and challenging to their intellect

Preferred Work Environments

- Contain independent thinkers focused on solving complex problems
- Allow privacy with plenty of time and space to think
- Foster independence and originality of thought
- Provide flexible policies and procedures
- Are quiet with as few meetings as possible
- Have unstructured and non-bureaucratic methods
- Reward self-determination

Potential Pitfalls

- May be too abstract and therefore unrealistic about necessary follow-through
- May overintellectualise and become too theoretical in their explanations
- May pay too much attention to minor inconsistencies at the expense of teamwork and harmony
- May turn their critical analytical thinking on people and act impersonally

Suggestions for Development

- May need to focus on practical details and develop concrete steps for implementation
- May need to state things more simply
- May need to yield on minor points in order to gain the cooperation of others
- May need to get to know more about others and express appreciation of them

ENTP

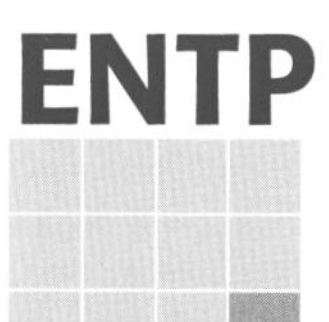

Extraverted Intuition with Thinking

ENTPs are innovative, strategic, versatile, analytical and entrepreneurial. They enjoy working with others in start-up activities that require ingenuity and unusual resourcefulness.

Contributions to the Organisation

- View limitations as challenges to be overcome
- Provide new ways to do things
- Bring a conceptual framework to problems
- Take initiative and spur others on
- Enjoy complex challenges that address future needs

Order of Preferences*
1 Intuition
2 Thinking
3 Feeling
4 Sensing

* *See pages 26–29 for further explanation.*

Leadership Style

- Plan theoretical systems to meet organisational needs
- Encourage independence in others
- Apply logic and find models for change
- Use compelling reasons for what they want to do
- Act as catalysts between people and systems

Problem-Solving Approach

- Want to explore future possibilities and patterns (N) and logically analyse the pros and cons for each (T)
- May need to include what people want and need (F) and the relevant facts and details (S) for optimal results

Preferred Learning Style

- Active, conceptual and expertly taught
- Challenging and big-picture-focused

Preferred Work Environments

- Contain independent people working on models to solve complicated problems
- Provide for flexibility and challenge
- Are change-oriented and non-bureaucratic
- Have competent people
- Reward risk taking
- Encourage autonomy and freedom of action
- Focus on the big picture

Potential Pitfalls

- May become lost in the model, forgetting about current realities and details
- May be competitive and unappreciative of the input of others
- May overextend themselves and experience burn-out
- May resist standard procedures and processes

Suggestions for Development

- May need to pay attention to the here and now and the essential facts
- May need to acknowledge and validate others' contributions
- May need to set realistic priorities and timescales and know when to stop
- May need to learn how to work within the system

ENTJ

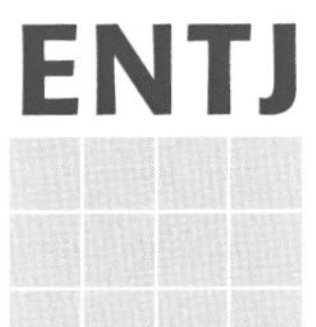

Extraverted Thinking with Intuition

ENTJs are logical, organised, structured, objective and decisive about what they view as conceptually valid. They enjoy working with others, especially when they can take charge and add a strategic plan.

Contributions to the Organisation

- Develop well-thought-out plans
- Provide structure to the organisation
- Design strategies that work towards broad goals
- Take charge quickly and do what it takes
- Deal directly with problems caused by confusion and inefficiency

Order of Preferences*

1 Thinking
2 Intuition
3 Sensing
4 Feeling

See pages 26–29 for further explanation.

Leadership Style

- Initiate an action-oriented, energetic approach
- Provide long-range plans to the organisation
- Manage directly – tough when necessary
- Enjoy complex problems and are resourceful in managing them
- Run as much of the organisation as possible

Problem-Solving Approach

- Want to logically analyse and control situations (T) based on an internal understanding of what could be (N)
- May want to include a realistic determination of the actual facts (S) and to consider the impact on people and themselves (F) for optimal results

Preferred Learning Style

- Cutting edge and theoretically based, delivered by experts
- Open to challenges and questions

Preferred Work Environments

- Contain results-oriented, independent and competent people focused on solving complex problems
- Are goal-oriented
- Have efficient systems and people
- Provide challenges with a direct payoff for effort
- Reward decisiveness
- Include tough-minded people
- Offer structure and focus on use of a master plan

Potential Pitfalls

- May overlook people's needs and contributions in their focus on the task
- May overlook pragmatic considerations and constraints
- May decide too quickly and appear impatient and domineering
- May ignore and suppress their own and others' feelings

Suggestions for Development

- May need to take account of the human element and appreciate others' contributions
- May need to check the practical, personal and situational resources available before plunging ahead
- May need to take time to reflect and consider all sides before deciding
- May need to learn to identify and value feelings in both themselves and others

Type Dynamics: Order of the Preferences

Besides being used as shorthand to indicate a set of preferences, the four-letter type code also stands for a complex set of dynamic relationships. Every person likes some of the preferences better than others. In fact, it is possible to predict the order in which any individual will develop, like and use their preferences. See page 28 for your type's order.

Dominant Function (no 1)

The middle two preferences (S–N and T–F) are referred to as *functions*. For each type, one of these four functions takes the lead, or is most preferred. This function is called the *dominant* function (or no 1 function). An analogy may help to illustrate the importance of the dominant function. No organisation can operate well without a sense of direction and purpose. The same holds true for a personality: few people can be effective or consistent without one of the functions taking the lead.

Effects of Extraversion and Introversion on the Dominant Function

People use their dominant function most in their favourite world. That is, if you are more energised by the external world (Extraversion), then that is where you use your dominant function. If you are more energised by the internal world (Introversion), then that is where you use your dominant function. So, Extraverts use their dominant function in their extraverted world, and Introverts use their dominant function in their introverted world. For example, ESTJs have extraverted Thinking as their dominant function; this means ESTJs typically offer their logical reasoning and conclusions out loud. On the other hand, ISTPs are also dominant Thinking types, but introverted Thinking is their dominant function. Therefore, ISTPs have a logical framework mostly in their heads ordering their thoughts. Other people may not always hear the reasons for their conclusions.

Auxiliary Function (no 2)

The other function in the type code (the other of the middle two letters) is called the *auxiliary* function (no 2) because it helps out and supports the dominant function. To continue the analogy, all organisations need at least two things to survive and be effective: good information and good decision making about that information. The same is true within each person. Thus, if a person uses the dominant function to bring in information (Sensing or Intuition), then the auxiliary function is used to make decisions about that information (Thinking or Feeling) and vice versa.

The Balancing Role of the Auxiliary Function

The auxiliary function helps to provide balance to our personality in another manner, providing ways to both act (extravert) and reflect (introvert). The dominant and auxiliary functions are used in opposite ways; if the dominant is extraverted, the auxiliary will be introverted. If the dominant function is introverted, the auxiliary will be extraverted. So for ESTJs, the information for their decisions comes from their introverted Sensing, that is, from their past experiences, information about what others have done, and so on. For ISTPs, the information for their introverted Thinking decisions comes from extraverted Sensing, what their current experience is and what others are doing.

Another way to think about this is to consider the leader of an organisation. Some leaders focus primarily on the outer world (Extraversion); they concentrate on those people or things in the environment that might affect the organisation. This kind of leader needs people to help maintain the internal (Introversion) functioning of the organisation. Other leaders prefer to direct their energies primarily to the internal (Introversion) organisation and delegate much of the external (Extraversion) monitoring to others.

Tertiary Function (no 3)

Even though they do not show up in the type code, everyone also uses the other two functions at times. The third, or *tertiary,* function is the preference opposite the auxiliary function. It may appear in both introverted or extraverted forms. For example, ESTJs use their tertiary function, Intuition, to see possibilities for the future of the organisation and to develop a vision around that future.

Inferior Function (no 4)

The *fourth,* or *inferior,* function (also called the *least-preferred* function) is the function opposite the dominant function. If the dominant function is extraverted, the fourth function will be introverted, and vice versa. It may be helpful to think about the fourth function as having two forms.

- **The *fourth* function is a way to tap into a deeper awareness of yourself, which will probably become more important to you at mid-life.** ESTJs, whose fourth function is introverted Feeling, will use the fourth function to tune into what is really important to them and others. They may become interested and involved in mentoring others and helping in the community. These actions tap into their least-preferred Feeling function, seeking ways to live out their values.
- **When people are under extreme stress, ill, or otherwise not acting like themselves, the fourth function may show up in negative ways and be experienced as the *inferior* function.** This means that for ESTJs the characteristics of introverted Feeling, such as knowing what is really important, take over the ESTJ's personality, but with a negative twist. For example, ESTJs may suddenly become hypersensitive and take things too personally, forgetting their usual logic. See page 29 for typical ways different types show their inferior function in these less-than-ideal circumstances.

Example

Putting it all together, consider INFPs (the opposite to ESTJs). INFPs' dominant function is Feeling. Because they prefer Introversion, their Feeling preference is used primarily in dealing with the inner world. Therefore, INFPs' probable focus is in deciding about ideas related to people using their internal, personally centred values. INFPs' auxiliary function is Intuition, which is used primarily in the outer world. Their auxiliary Intuition function provides ideas and possibilities to help them make decisions. The tertiary function is Sensing; the inferior function is Thinking. INFPs might choose to delve into the logic of the situation, such as involvement in academic or scholarly pursuits. When under stress, INFPs may have difficulty identifying the applicable logical principles.

In MBTI terms, the order of preferences for the INFP is

Dominant	=	1 Feeling (Introverted)
Auxiliary	=	2 Intuition (Extraverted)
Tertiary	=	3 Sensing (Extraverted or Introverted)
Inferior	=	4 Thinking (Extraverted)

A Note on Introversion

Remember, Introverts are more likely to show their auxiliary function to others because their dominant function is used mainly inside, in their favoured introverted world. What you see with Introverted types is not always what is most important to them. For example, INTJs often show others their extraverted Thinking with its characteristics of logical structure and analysis. Others may not realise that the INTJ's dominant introverted Intuition with its vision for future possibilities is really in charge.

People may experience IJs (the top row in the type table) as having their minds made up because they use their deciding function (Thinking or Feeling) in the external world. IPs (the second row in the type table) may seem more adaptable than they actually are on a given issue because they extravert their perceiving or data-gathering function (Sensing or Intuition).

Order of the Preferences for Each Type

ISTJ	ISFJ	INFJ	INTJ
1 Sensing (I)	1 Sensing (I)	1 Intuition (I)	1 Intuition (I)
2 Thinking (E)	2 Feeling (E)	2 Feeling (E)	2 Thinking (E)
3 Feeling (E or I)	3 Thinking (E or I)	3 Thinking (E or I)	3 Feeling (E or I)
4 Intuition (E)	4 Intuition (E)	4 Sensing (E)	4 Sensing (E)
ISTP	**ISFP**	**INFP**	**INTP**
1 Thinking (I)	1 Feeling (I)	1 Feeling (I)	1 Thinking (I)
2 Sensing (E)	2 Sensing (E)	2 Intuition (E)	2 Intuition (E)
3 Intuition (E or I)	3 Intuition (E or I)	3 Sensing (E or I)	3 Sensing (E or I)
4 Feeling (E)	4 Thinking (E)	4 Thinking (E)	4 Feeling (E)
ESTP	**ESFP**	**ENFP**	**ENTP**
1 Sensing (E)	1 Sensing (E)	1 Intuition (E)	1 Intuition (E)
2 Thinking (I)	2 Feeling (I)	2 Feeling (I)	2 Thinking (I)
3 Feeling (E or I)	3 Thinking (E or I)	3 Thinking (E or I)	3 Feeling (E or I)
4 Intuition (I)	4 Intuition (I)	4 Sensing (I)	4 Sensing (I)
ESTJ	**ESFJ**	**ENFJ**	**ENTJ**
1 Thinking (E)	1 Feeling (E)	1 Feeling (E)	1 Thinking (E)
2 Sensing (I)	2 Sensing (I)	2 Intuition (I)	2 Intuition (I)
3 Intuition (E or I)	3 Intuition (E or I)	3 Sensing (E or I)	3 Sensing (E or I)
4 Feeling (I)	4 Thinking (I)	4 Thinking (I)	4 Feeling (I)

How to Help Those Experiencing Their Inferior Function

When Sensing and Intuitive dominant types are using their fourth functions in negative or inferior ways, encourage them to take a break. Then invite them to consider which facts and possibilities are the most logical and/or the most important ones to act on – in other words, use their auxiliary and tertiary functions of Thinking or Feeling.

When Thinking and Feeling dominant types are using their fourth functions in negative or inferior ways, encourage them to take a break. Then invite them to gather the relevant facts and/or consider possible options – in other words, use their auxiliary and tertiary functions of Sensing or Intuition.

Characteristics and Consequences of the Dominant (no 1) and Inferior (no 4) Functions

When **Sensing is no 1** (dominant) and **Intuition is no 4** (inferior), as in ISTJ, ISFJ, ESTP and ESFP, you are likely to have the ***clearest awareness of what is.***

You are likely to

- Recognise the pertinent facts
- Apply experience to problems
- Notice what needs attention
- Keep track of essentials
- Handle problems with realism

Under stress, you may

- Become caught in a rut rehashing the same details
- Get stuck, not use common sense, and not see possible ways out
- View the future in negative terms
- Become unduly pessimistic

When **Intuition is no 1** (dominant) and **Sensing is no 4** (inferior), as in INTJ, INFJ, ENTP and ENFP, you are likely to have the ***clearest awareness of what could be.***

You are likely to

- Recognise new possibilities
- Come up with novel solutions to problems
- Delight in focusing on the future
- Be on the lookout for additional ideas
- Tackle new problems with zest

Under stress, you may

- Become overwhelmed with ideas and possibilities, all equally enticing
- Get obsessed with unimportant details
- Become preoccupied with one irrelevant fact, making it represent the entire domain
- Overindulge in sensory pursuits, e.g. eating, drinking, watching TV, or exercising too much

When **Thinking is no 1** (dominant) and **Feeling is no 4** (inferior), as in ISTP, INTP, ESTJ and ENTJ, you are likely to have the ***clearest awareness of what is logical.***

You are likely to

- Analyse the situation
- Find flaws in advance
- Hold consistently to a principle
- Weigh up "the law and the evidence"
- Stand firm against opposition

Under stress, you may

- Become opinionated to the point of becoming unreasonable
- Have uncontrolled emotional outbursts and show anger or other emotions unexpectedly
- Be hypersensitive to "suspected" slights
- Take criticism very personally

When **Feeling is no 1** (dominant) and **Thinking is no 4** (inferior), as in ISFP, INFP, ESFJ and ENFJ, you are likely to have the ***clearest awareness of what matters.***

You are likely to

- Empathise with people
- Be concerned about how others will feel
- Allow for extenuating circumstances
- Know what is really important
- Appreciate each person's contributions

Under stress, you may

- Stop listening to and accommodating others
- Become so sensitive to conflict, you ignore or avoid it
- Be hypercritical; find fault with almost everything, but in an illogical manner
- Act overly domineering, taking charge without listening to others

Remember, if you have a preference for Extraversion (E) you often show the characteristics of your dominant function, as in the left-hand column above, to others. If you have a preference for Introversion (I) you often use these characteristics internally; therefore, they may be less evident to others. As a general rule, this may mean you need to work harder to communicate this information to others.

Remember, the inferior function shows itself typically in this form (see right-hand column) when you are under stress, ill or fatigued. These are only a few of the more common forms of the inferior function.

Left column adapted from Myers, 1962.

Decision-Making Process Using Type Preferences

The MBTI preferences can be helpful when working on problems and making decisions, for both individuals and teams. Although this process seems straightforward, it can actually be difficult to fully implement because people have a tendency to skip over the parts of the process that require them to use their less-preferred (no 3 and no 4) functions.

Decisions are usually made by emphasising your dominant function and ignoring your least-preferred function. A better decision is likely to result if all of the preferences are used.

The problem-solving model is below. The model is a circle to show that you can begin at any point and move in any direction, according to your own order of preferences. You are likely to start with your dominant (no 1) function, proceed to your auxiliary (no 2) function, and pay scant attention to your third and fourth functions.

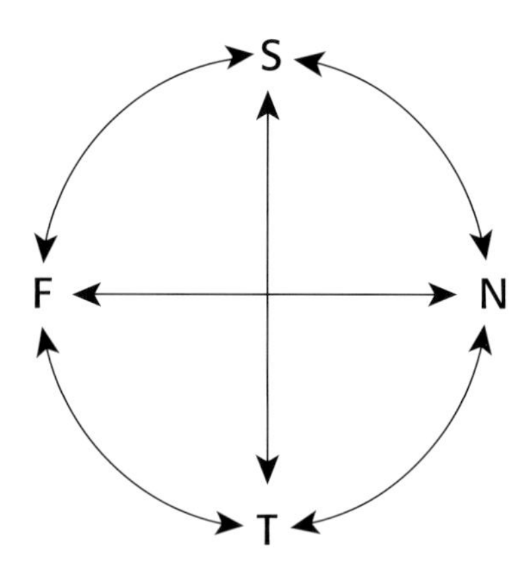

Model adapted from the works of Isabel Briggs Myers.

Covering All the Bases

By paying attention to all four functions, a better solution results. Ultimately, all points in the circle need to be covered. Asking (and answering) the questions listed on the following page can be one way of covering all the bases.

For example, ENFPs may search for the possibilities (no 1 N), then consider their importance (no 2 F). Ideally, they will continue by considering the logic (no 3 T) and the facts (no 4 S).

Until you master this process, it might be wise for you to consult others of opposite preferences when making important decisions, or to pay particular attention to the contributions of your own third or fourth functions. Likewise, if a team is overloaded with certain types, pay particular attention to the preferences that are missing. Similarly, consultations with others of different types may prove beneficial.

Questions to Ask of Each Preference

Sensing (S)

- How did we get into this situation?
- What are the verifiable facts?
- What exactly is the situation now?
- What has been done and by whom?
- What already exists and works?

Intuition (N)

- What interpretations can be made from the facts?
- What insights and hunches come to mind about this situation?
- What would the possibilities be if there were no restrictions?
- What other directions/fields can be explored?
- What is this problem analogous to?

Thinking (T)

- What are the pros and cons of each alternative?
- What are the logical consequences of the options?
- What are the objective criteria that need to be satisfied?
- What are the costs of each choice?
- What is the most reasonable course of action?

Feeling (F)

- How will the outcome affect the people, the process and/or the organisation?
- What is my personal reaction to (my likes and dislikes about) each alternative?
- How will others react and respond to the options?
- What are the underlying values involved for each choice?
- Who is committed to carrying out the solution?

Finally, follow these steps:

- Use Introversion (I) to allow time for reflection at each step along the way.
- Use Extraversion (E) to discuss each step before moving on.
- Use Perceiving (P) in each step to keep discussions and options open, not cutting things off prematurely.
- Then use Judging (J) to make a decision and determine a deadline and schedule.

Using Your Natural Strengths

Although any type can perform any role, each type tends to gravitate towards particular styles. You function best when you can adopt a style that allows you to express your own preferences. When you are forced to use a style over a long period of time that does not allow for, or call upon, your preferences, inefficiency and burn-out may result. So, although you can adopt a different style when needed and call upon different preferences when appropriate, you will contribute most when you are using your own preferences. Basically, our message is:
GO WITH YOUR STRENGTHS.

Steps for Further Understanding

MBTI Step II

The MBTI Step II is another method of scoring the MBTI and presenting your results. It yields the four basic preferences described in this booklet and 20 ways in which you express your type. For example, we often expect people who prefer Extraversion to do a lot of talking. But occasionally, those who prefer Introversion like to do this as well. Introverts who exhibit this behaviour would be considered Expressive Introverts. Likewise, there are some Extraverts who prefer to keep their thoughts to themselves; they are called Contained Extraverts. (In Step II, Expressive and Contained are two opposite facets of Extraversion and Introversion.) The Step II Expanded Interpretive Report provides in-depth detail about each individual's variations within his or her type.

Further Reading

Barger, Nancy J., & Kirby, Linda K. (1995). *The Challenge of Change in Organizations.* Mountain View, CA: Davies-Black.

Brock, Susan A. (1994). *Using Type in Selling: Building Customer Relationships with the Myers-Briggs Type Indicator.* Mountain View, CA: CPP, Inc.

Hammer, Allen L. (1993). *Introduction to Type and Careers.* Mountain View, CA: CPP, Inc.

Hirsh, Sandra K. (1992). *Introduction to Type and Teams.* Mountain View, CA: CPP, Inc.

Hirsh, Sandra K., with Kise, Jane. (1997). *Work it Out!* Mountain View, CA: Davies-Black.

Hirsh, Sandra K., & Kummerow, Jean M. (1989). *LIFETypes.* New York: Warner Books.

Kummerow, Jean M., Barger, Nancy J., & Kirby, Linda K. (1997). *WORKTypes.* New York: Warner Books.

Myers, Isabel B. (1998). *Introduction to Type* (Sixth Edition). Mountain View, CA: CPP, Inc.

Myers, Katharine D., & Kirby, Linda K. (1994). *Introduction to Type Dynamics and Development: Exploring the Next Level of Type.* Mountain View, CA: CPP, Inc.

Pearman, Roger R., & Albritton, Sarah C. (1997). *I'm Not Crazy, I'm Just Not You.* Mountain View, CA: Davies-Black.

Quenk, Naomi L. (1996). *In the Grip: Understanding Type, Stress and the Inferior Function.* Mountain View, CA: CPP, Inc.

Most of these materials are available from:
OPP Ltd, Elsfield Hall, 15–17 Elsfield Way, Oxford, OX2 8EP, UK.

For further information or to place an order telephone +44 (0) 845 603 9958.